GREAT BIG
WORLD OF COMPUTERS-
HISTORY AND EVOLUTION:
5TH GRADE SCIENCE SERIES

SPEEDY
PUBLISHING

Speedy Publishing LLC
40 E. Main St. #1156
Newark, DE 19711
www.speedypublishing.com

A computer is a general-purpose device that can be programmed to carry out a set of arithmetic or logical operations automatically.

The abacus was initially used for arithmetic tasks. The abacus is the most ancient calculating device known. The abacus is also called a counting frame.

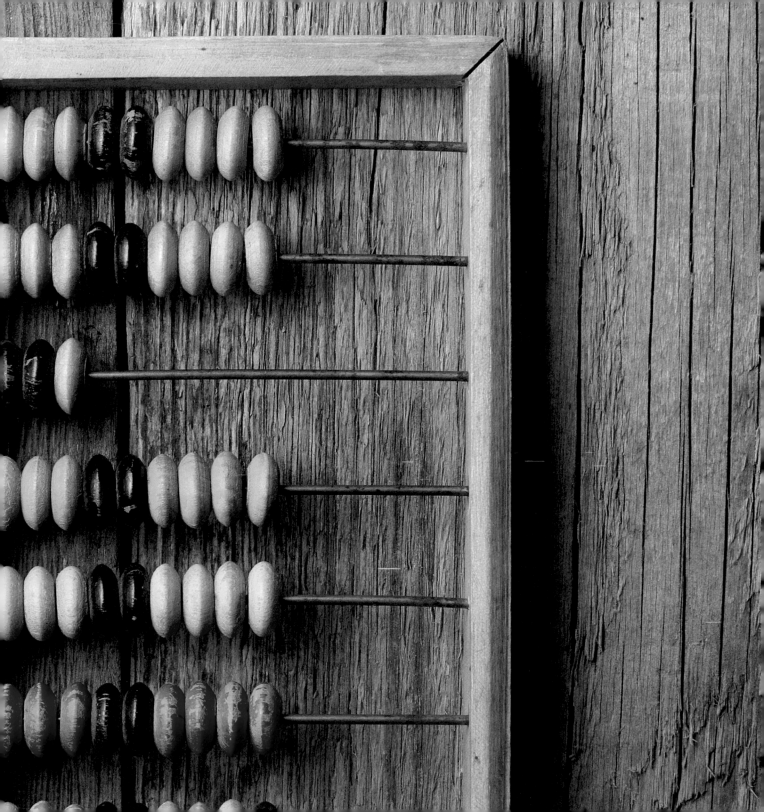

Charles Babbage originated the concept of a programmable computer. His machines were considered as one of the very first mechanical computers ever to be invented. He is considered a "father of the computer".

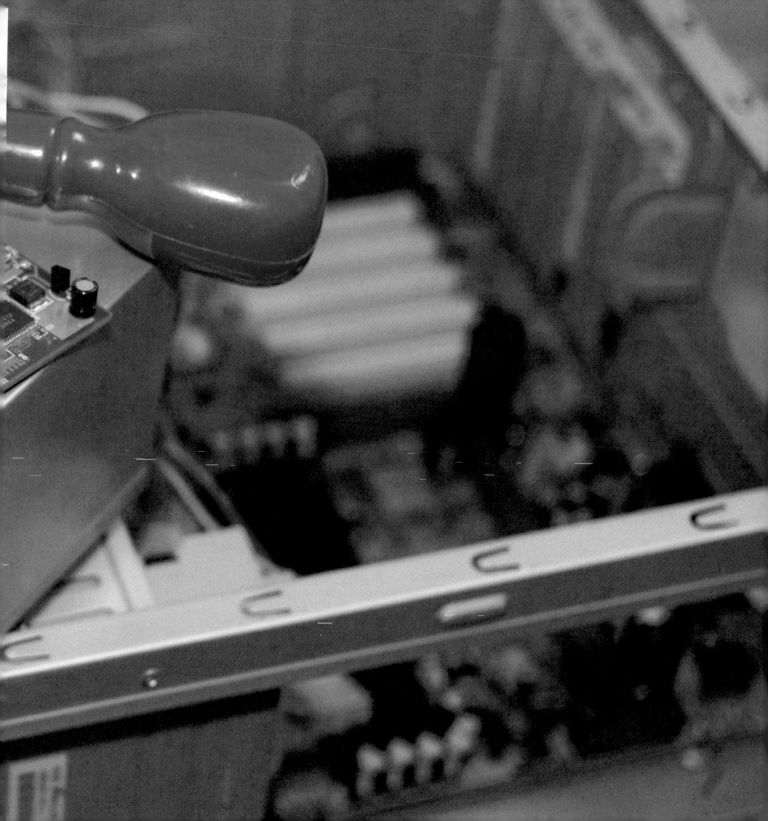

Early electronic computers, developed around the 1940's, were the size of a large room and consumed huge amounts of electricity.

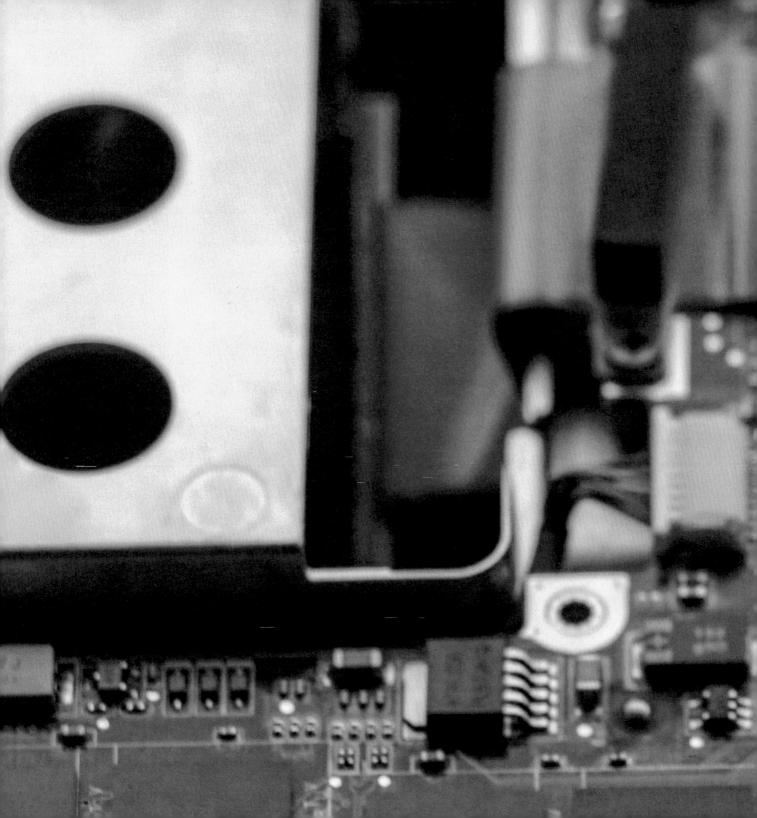

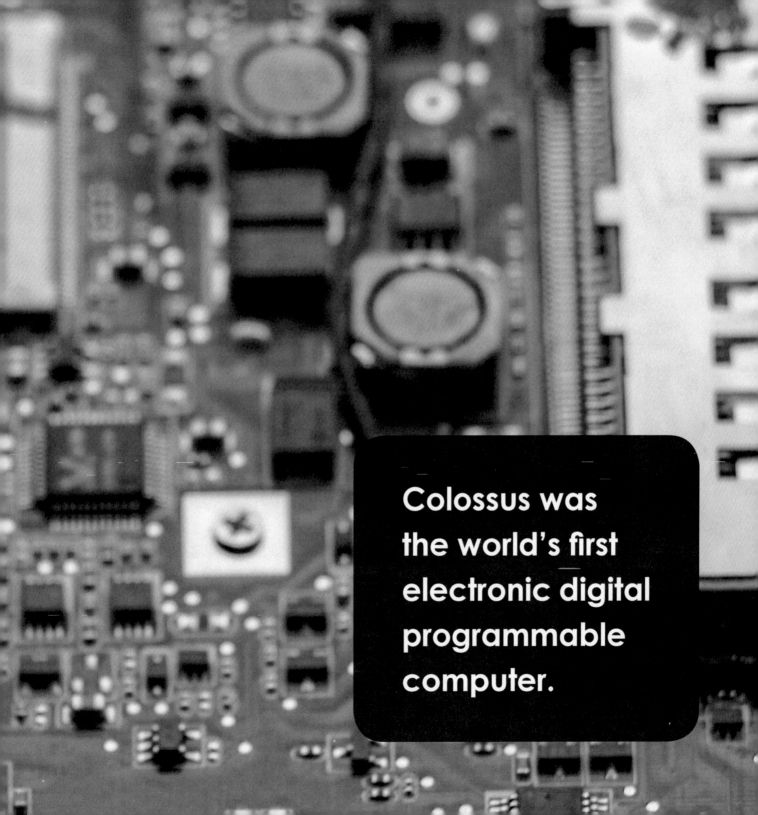

Colossus was the world's first electronic digital programmable computer.

Computers as we know them today only really started being made in 1980.

Computers interact with a number of different devices to exchange information. These devices include the keyboard, mouse, display, hard drive, printer and more.

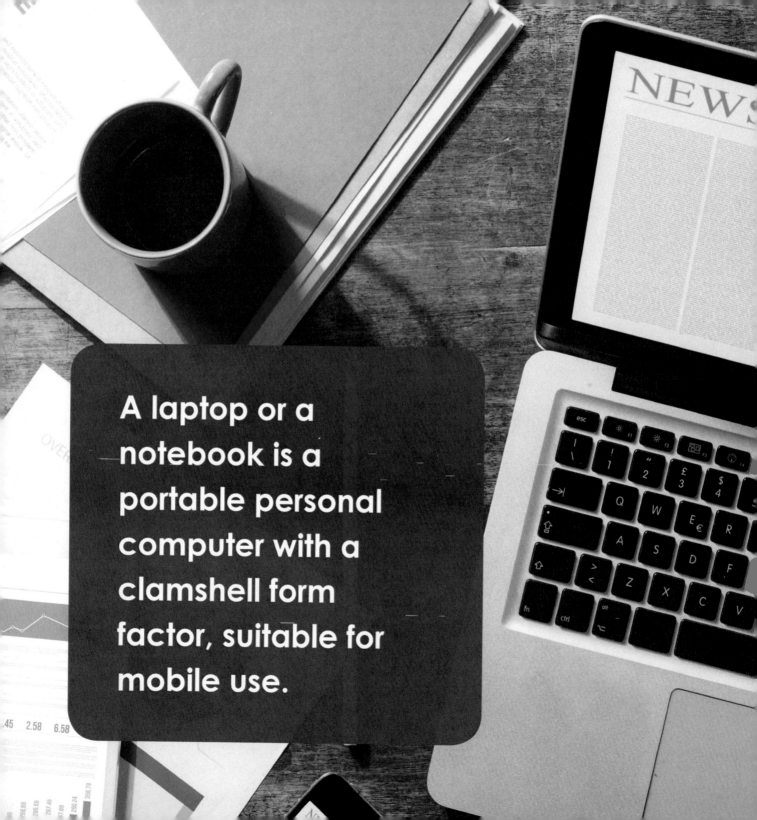

A laptop or a notebook is a portable personal computer with a clamshell form factor, suitable for mobile use.

Made in the USA
San Bernardino, CA
15 November 2018